31 Days to
Transform Your Life

A Daily Action Guide for
Increasing
Joy, Satisfaction and Fulfillment

31 Days to Transform Your Life

A Daily Action Guide for Increasing Joy, Satisfaction and Fulfillment

Lisa Giruzzi

Design Credits:

Cover Design & Art Direction
Brian Penry | penrycreative.com

Cover Concept
Rosemary Naftalis

Photo of Author
Joan Heffler | www.joanheffler.com

Book Text Design
Eric R. Mead

Published by
Transformational Conversations
6 Oakmont Terrace
Albany, NY 12205

www.TransformationalConversations.com

Book sales contact:
info@TransformationalConversations.com
888-330-8288

ISBN – 978-0-615-30350-5

Library of Congress Control Number: 2009933786

Transformational Checklist

Foreword

"No problem can be solved from the same level of consciousness that created it. We must learn to see the world anew."

– Albert Einstein, Physicist, Nobel Prize Winner

In 1992, I was in a very high-pressure career working for a local government agency. One day, I was walking by a friend's cubicle just as he was speaking with a new hire. He was giving her the "lay of the land." I was just about to walk in when I heard him say to her, "Be sure to watch out for Lisa and Mary. They are good people but they can be nasty and abrasive."

I stopped dead in my tracks. I knew *Mary* was like that, but *me*? Not *me*? If it had been anyone else speaking, I probably would have lost my temper (which, of course, would only prove him right) and, ultimately, I would have discounted his opinion. Instead, because of how much I trusted and respected my friend, I thought for a moment, "What if what he is saying is true?"

In that moment I saw myself through his eyes and I had a transformational experience. I could see that who I had become was not who I wanted to be. Before that moment, I was unconscious to the person I had become and was living my life oblivious to the impact I was having on others. Seeing my friend's perspective allowed me to make a choice to either continue on the path I was on or to change, to be the person I *really* wanted to be. This began my journey in transformation.

I titled this book "31 Days to Transform Your Life" because I believe that it offers you an opportunity to see yourself and your life from a new perspective, to have your eyes opened as mine were on that day back in 1992.

Since then, I have immersed myself in transformational work. I have done numerous programs, read a multitude of books, worked for a transformational education company, studied many disciplines, led transformational programs and worked with thousands of people to assist them in transforming their lives. This book is a compilation of what I've learned in the last 17 years since that day my eyes were opened; it contains the essential elements that I believe are necessary to significantly enhance the quality of your life.

This book was designed to be simple yet profound. Read the book, do the activities and, most importantly, be open to "seeing the world anew." You will be astounded by the transformation that occurs and the positive difference it will make in your life.

— Lisa Giruzzi
2009

To my wonderful husband, Bill, with love.

Introduction

"To change one's life: Start immediately. Do it flamboyantly. No exceptions."

– William James, Philosopher

If you have picked up this book, chances are you are looking for a change. Perhaps you are dissatisfied with your life, in some way. Or maybe you are someone who is restless, always looking for a way to improve your quality of life. Or, maybe you have made significant changes on your own – stopped smoking, lost weight, etc. – and now you are looking for what's next. No matter. Whatever the reason you picked up this book, it is my commitment that you will achieve the change you seek.

This book can be a guide to transforming your life. However, merely holding it in your hand will not cause a transformation; reading it and engaging in the "Transformational Actions" outlined in the following pages will. There are 31 lessons in this book. Any one of them has the power to transform your life. Putting them all together will increase the power of your transformation exponentially.

Some of the "Transformational Actions" may seem easy while others may be more challenging. If your reaction to an action is, "I don't want to," there is a good chance doing it is essential for you to have a breakthrough. On the other hand, if your reaction is, "This feels *wrong for me,"* or *"unsafe,"* then trust your instincts. You can always come back to it at another time.

The lessons do not have to be done in order however; I recommend that you do the Day One lesson first. They also do not have to be done in a one-month period. There are bonus activities for some of the days to further enhance the impact of your transformation. Additionally, I encourage you to incorporate the "Transformational Actions" that you find most valuable into daily or weekly practices to support your ongoing journey. Recording any insights, breakthroughs, i.e., "Aha!" moments – in a journal will further add to your experience.

The most important thing is for you to make the commitment to accomplish all the lessons and choose a completion date. Then give it your best shot. Enjoy the process. Transformation can be an absolute blast if you allow it to be.

Another suggestion I have is to get a friend or partner to take this journey with you. In my 20-plus years of working with people, I have found that those who have someone to support and someone who supports them are far more likely to fulfill their goals. It is too easy to blow off promises we make to ourselves. "I'll do it tomorrow," we tell ourselves. When we make promises to a partner we are more likely to keep them. We also get satisfaction out of helping someone else achieve success.

Finally, one last bit of coaching: **YOU** have a choice. Someone once said to me, "You either have the results you want or the reasons why not; choose." Which would *you* rather have, the results or your reasons? Choose!

Here's to your results!!

Notes:

Day 1
Question Your Perspective

"Everyone is a prisoner of his own experiences. No one can eliminate prejudices - just recognize them."

– Edward R. Murrow, American Broadcast Journalist

Each of us has a unique perspective on life, comprised of our past experiences. We also have amassed tons of proof that our version of reality is the right or true one. What if your perspective is only one possible interpretation of the world? It is not right or wrong or true or false. It is just one of many possible explanations. What if all of them are valid but not true?

Transformational Actions:

1. Pick a topic or an area of your life and ask yourself the following questions:
    - Do I believe my perspective is the right or true one?
    - How does this impact my life? My relationships?
    - Where did I get my perspective?
    - How else can I think about the situation to give me more of what I want?

2. Find someone whose perspective differs from yours. Tell them you are curious and ask to interview them, using the following questions (only ask questions, no debating):
    - How did you come to that conclusion?
    - What makes this true for you?
    - How does this view of the situation serve you?

3. Reflect on the experience. What did you learn?

Notes:

Day 2
Focus On Your Successes

"Your life is an occasion; rise to it."

– Mr. Magorium, as played by Dustin Hoffman in
"Mr. Magorium's Wonder Emporium"

We live in a world where focusing on weaknesses and trying to fix what's wrong is the primary mode of thinking. We have been led to believe that the access to greatness is through improving our weaknesses.

This is a myth. Consider that the access to greatness is through focusing on your talents and strengths and making your weaknesses irrelevant. The most successful people in the world know this. Our greatest learning comes from our areas of strength. It's time to discover your source of power.

Transformational Actions:

1. Reflect back over your life. Make a list of 20 to 25 high point experiences – both personal and professional: times when you felt happy, satisfied, engaged, enlivened and/or proud of yourself and your accomplishment. Each item on the list should be a separate period of time or event, i.e., a great conversation with a colleague, a project you worked on, a vacation, a graduation, etc.

2. Reflect on the experience. What did you learn?

Notes:

Day 3
Learn From Your Successes

"Success leaves clues."

– James Malinchak, Motivational Speaker, Entrepreneur

There is much to discover from the times when you have succeeded. When you can reveal the elements that led to a success, you can replicate them for the future, building a pathway toward what you want and increasing the odds for future successes.

Transformational Actions:

1. Review the list of 20 to 25 high point experiences from Day 2. For each situation, answer the following two questions:
    a. What was it about **you** that made the high point experience possible?

    b. What was it about the **situation** that made the high point experience possible?

2. What themes or patterns emerge? Make a list of these themes.

3. These are the conditions under which you work best. What does knowing this information make possible for your future?

Notes:

Day 4
Smile!

"Sometimes your joy is the source of your smile, but sometimes your smile can be the source of your joy."

– Thich Nhat Hanh, Zen Master, Poet, Peace Activist

For most people, smiling is a reaction to something external. That's one way to smile. Another is to smile as a reaction to something internal. Thinking about one of your successes, a happy memory or even dreaming of a positive future can cause a smile.

What about smiling just for the sake of smiling? Merely smiling improves a person's outlook and sense of happiness. Additionally, smiling acts like a magnet and draws more positivity to you. Smiling may seem trite or clichéd but the impact of deliberately smiling more can be quite profound.

Transformational Actions:

1.   Visit a humor Web Site such as www.ajokeaday.com. Read through the jokes for the last seven days.

2.   Spend five minutes reflecting on something that has made you happy. Really put yourself in the moment of it and relive it.

3.   Set an alarm to go off once per hour. When it goes off, check to see if you are smiling. If you are not, SMILE!

Notes:

Day 5
Stop the Blame Game

"Take your life in your own hands and what happens? A terrible thing: No one to blame."

– Erica Jong, Author

The concept of cause and effect is an illusion. There is always more to the story than we know. If a boulder rolls down a hill and crashes into a fence, one could say the boulder caused the broken fence. But what made the boulder roll? If someone pushed it, are they the cause of the broken fence? But what if someone pushed them into the boulder? There is *always* something that came before.

What if what you think is the *cause* of your *circumstances* is all an illusion? What if what you think is the *cause* of how you *feel* is all an illusion? What if there is more to the story than you know? Perhaps access to true power is declaring that *you* are the "cause" of your own life.

Transformational Actions:

1. Think about a situation where you blame someone or something for the way it is.

2. Ask yourself the following questions:
   - What is the impact on my life of blaming something or someone else for the situation?
   - What was my role in the situation?
   - If I were the cause of my own life, i.e., took responsibility for how it is, what would I do to resolve the situation?

3. For one whole day, take on the perspective that *you* are the cause of your own life. Notice how it changes your thoughts and actions.

Notes:

Day 6
What's Your Story?

"I have been through some terrible things in my life, some of which actually happened."

– Mark Twain, Humorist, Novelist, Short Story Author and Wit

From early childhood each of us has been weaving the story of our life. The problem is, we forgot *we* were the ones weaving it. Lots of things happened to us over the years and our point of view shaped and colored all of it. *We* decided if something was good or bad. *We* decided who were the heroes, the villains and the extras. *We* made all of these decisions. The unfortunate thing is that we get so enamored of our version of reality that we miss out on everything that doesn't agree with it. Imagine what would happen if you did not have to keep living the same old story. What if you could start writing a new story? Perhaps an adventure, a romance or maybe even one that ends happily ever after.

Transformational Actions:

1. Write the current story of your life. Use as many pages as you need to tell the whole story.

2. Read it five times and then rip it to shreds or burn it.

3. Write a new story of your life, how you want it to be from this day forward.

4. Start living your new story today.

Notes:

Day 7
Whom Do You Admire?

"Admiration, n.: Our polite recognition of another's resemblance to ourselves."

– Ambrose Bierce, Author and Satirist

The people we *choose* to admire says something about us. There are thousands of people we come in contact with, read about or hear about throughout the course of our lives. Yet only the traits of certain people stand out and strike us as worthy of admiration. Why?

The standard belief is that people admire who they are not, i.e., the traits or qualities they wish they had. Perhaps it is the opposite. Perhaps we admire the people we resemble in some way; we see ourselves in them. Discovering who we are in awe of reveals our own greatness.

Transformational Actions:

1. Make a list of five people you admire and why.

2. Choose at least one person from your list and interview them. See Appendix A for sample interview questions. Even if the person is someone you do not know, contact him or her to request an interview.

3. After the interview, review your list of themes from the exercise on Day 3. Look for similarities between you and the person you interviewed.

Notes:

Day 8
You Are Admired

"Appreciation is a wonderful thing: It makes what is excellent in others belong to us as well."

– Voltaire, French Author, Humanist, Rationalist, and Satirist

You are admired. Let that sink in for a minute. There is at least one person who admires YOU. Someone who thinks you are great and wishes they were more like you! How does it make you feel to know that you are admired? There is much to learn from seeing yourself through the eyes of your admirer. Are you willing to see it?

Transformational Actions:

1. Think about the people in your life and make a list of five people you *think* might admire you. (It does not matter if they do or don't.)

2. Choose one person from your list and interview them. See Appendix B for sample interview questions.

3. Make a list of *at least* five things you learned from this interview.

Notes:

Day 9
Give Beyond Reason

"If you knew what I know about the power of giving, you would not let a single meal pass without sharing it in some way."

– Buddha, Philosopher and Religious Leader

Generosity is transformational. When you fill a need for someone else, when you know *you* were the one who made the difference, when you lightened the load for someone and you did not have to, it is confirmation that you matter, that your existence means something. Generosity for generosity's sake is a beautiful thing to behold and is wonderfully life affirming for everyone involved.

Transformational Actions:

1. Make a list of five things you could do as an act of generosity. This is not about anonymously donating money to an organization. This is about performing some act that will make a difference for someone; giving of yourself, i.e., shoveling your neighbor's driveway, watching your neighbor's children so the parents can go out on a date, reading to an elderly person, etc.

2. Pick one of the actions and do it.

***Bonus: Do all five.

Notes:

Day 10
Dream

"The future belongs to those who believe in the beauty of their dreams."

– Eleanor Roosevelt, First Lady, Diplomat and Activist

Did you know there is no future? Really think about this. You are always in the present moment. We think and talk about the future as if it is fixed in stone or has some independent reality but, in fact, there is no future. Tomorrow at this time will be just another "now" when you get there.

This is great news! If there really is no future that means you can create it. It is your vision of the future that influences your present moment. The future you imagine gives you your experience now. Imagine an all-expense-paid afternoon at the spa, and then imagine being at work. Each gives you a different experience in this moment.

Dreaming of the future, imagining something you really want, something you do not know how to achieve but would make you wildly happy if you got it, that's the kind of dream that changes your life.

Transformational Actions:

1. Imagine you awaken tomorrow to find it is five years in the future. As if by magic, your life and the world have changed in all the ways you most wanted it to. What would it be like? What would be the same? What would be different? (If your dream involves being rich or getting money, ask yourself what would the money provide; delve deeper.)

2. Write out your dream as if you're writing a journal or diary entry – like it has happened already. What does it feel like to live in this new reality? Who have you become as a result of achieving this dream?

3. Live today as if your dream has already happened, i.e., take on the persona of the person you would be if your dream were realized.

Notes:

Day 11
Appreciate Your Life

"If you look at what you have in life, you'll always have more. If you look at what you don't have in life, you'll never have enough."

– Oprah Winfrey, Television Talk Show Host, Actress and Philanthropist

What do you love about your life? What's working about your life? In what way are things perfect? All these questions are intended to get you to focus on what you appreciate about your life.

On any given day, there is a lot to appreciate. Maybe it is your warm bed or a great friendship or your health. Even the situations and circumstances you do not want can be opportunities to appreciate. Perhaps a challenging relationship is teaching you patience or financial struggles are challenging you to grow.

Being appreciative of something doesn't mean you do not want it to change. It simply means you are accepting the way that it is and are grateful for the experience. Until you can appreciate and accept something, it is virtually impossible to change.

Transformational Actions:

1. Make a list of 25 things you appreciate about yourself and your life.

***Bonus: Come up with 25 more.

2. For each of your significant relationships, list three things you appreciate about them.

Notes:

Day 12
Check Your Listening

"If the person you are talking to doesn't appear to be listening, be patient. It may simply be that he has a small piece of fluff in his ear."

– "Pooh's Little Instruction Book,"
Inspired by A. A. Milne

We all listen differently, based on our beliefs, opinions, past experiences, etc. Yet, we barely put any attention on how we listen.

We also listen differently in different situations. Imagine being on an airplane and the flight attendant is giving routine safety instructions. How do you listen? What if during the flight there is engine failure and the pilot directs the flight attendant to go over the safety instructions again? *Now* how do you listen?

The way we listen impacts everything. We have the power to alter how we listen at any given moment in time. We can choose to listen with compassion, with intention, with love, or we can listen to learn, or to appreciate. Choose how to listen and you will have the power to transform everything.

Transformational Actions:

1. Ask yourself throughout the course of your day, "How am I listening right now?"

2. Think about how you want people to listen to you, and then listen that way to others.

Notes:

Day 13
Breathe!

"Breathe. Let go. And remind yourself that this very moment is the only one you know you have for sure."

– Oprah Winfrey, Television Talk Show Host, Actress and Philanthropist

Reminding you to breathe may sound ridiculous since breathing comes naturally to us but consider that for the most part the way you breathe is insufficient for maximum performance.

There are two levels to this lesson. First, most people do not breathe deeply enough. We take shallow breaths and this impacts every area of our functioning. Not getting enough oxygen to the brain and other areas of the body is detrimental to our overall health.

Second, by focusing on your breathing, you allow yourself to slow down and get present to the moment. It is so easy to get caught up in the craziness of our lives. Days go by and we feel like we missed them. Consciously putting your attention on your breathing is an easy way to "show up" in your own life.

Transformational Actions:

1. Pick four times during the day (e.g., morning, noon, dinner and bed), and take 10 slow, deep breaths. Think: Smell the flowers and blow out the candles.

2. As you are breathing, relax your neck and shoulders; focus on each breath.

3. Notice any changes in your body, thoughts and feelings.

Notes:

Day 14
Practice Not Knowing

"The greatest obstacle to discovering the shape of the Earth, the continents, and the ocean was not ignorance but the illusion of knowledge."

– Daniel J. Boorstin, Historian, Professor, Attorney and Writer

Knowledge can be a beautiful thing. It can also be a huge hindrance. Have you ever tried to have a conversation with someone who thinks he or she knows it all? It can be incredibly frustrating.

We all have that tendency, to a certain degree. In areas where we believe we already know the answers, we stop learning and wondering. Knowledge can cause us to miss new information or it can get in the way of our creativity.

It is not that knowledge is bad, it's that when we settle on answers, we stop looking for new possibilities in life. Wonder, inquiry and discovery open you up to life, to new possibilities and to new experiences.

Transformational Actions:

1. Answer all the questions that you are asked today with, "I don't know. What do you think?" even if you do know the answer.

2. Listen to learn today. Approach situations from the perspective, "What can I learn from this?"

Notes:

Day 15
You Are So Amazing

"Appreciation can make a day, even change a life. Your willingness to put it into words is all that is necessary."

– Margaret Cousins, Author

There is nothing like a good acknowledgement. You know the kind – when you feel truly *known* afterward. It is as if the person who acknowledged you got to the heart of who you are. It went beyond a compliment and captured your essence. This kind of acknowledgement has real power in it. It goes beyond "feeling good" to affirming your value. It allows you to authentically be who you are.

Transformational Actions:

1. Make a list of five people in your life that you care about and, for each person, write one thing that you appreciate about them.

2. Acknowledge each of the people on the list. Start the acknowledgement with the phrase, "You know what I really appreciate about you?" and then tell them.

***Bonus: Acknowledge a person that you do not like or have issues with, in the same manner as above.

Notes:

Day 16
Accept Your Gifts

"Every time we remember to say 'thank you,' we experience nothing less than heaven on earth."

– Sarah Ban Breathnach, Author

One of the simplest things you can do to accept your greatness is to say "thank you" when someone compliments or acknowledges you. And not some quick, insincere thank you. A real "look 'em in the eye, I appreciate your making the effort to acknowledge me" kind of thank you.

It will make both you and the person acknowledging you feel great. Saying thank you like you mean it allows you to truly accept your gifts and allows the person acknowledging you to feel good about appreciating you.

Transformational Actions:

1.   For one whole day, respond to all compliments and acknowledgements with a sincere thank you. Do not say anything except thank you.

2.   After you say thank you, listen to what you say to yourself. This is your attempt to deflect the compliment. Tell your "little voice" to be quiet and dwell in the compliment.

Notes:

Day 17
Laugh Out Loud

"Those who can laugh without cause have either found the true meaning of happiness or have gone stark raving mad."

– Norm Papernick, Comedian

Everyone knows that laughing is good for you. It relieves stress and tension and creates connections between people. But how often do we intentionally seek out laughter? Most of the time, laughter is a reaction to something external.

Taking control and choosing opportunities to laugh is a wonderful thing to do. Whether you watch funny movies, listen to your favorite comedian, or get together with friends to share funny stories, committing to more laughter will change your life.

Transformational Actions:

1. Ask five people, "What is the funniest movie you ever saw, and why?" Ask them to describe the funniest scene they remember.

2. Watch a funny movie or listen to a comedian.

Notes:

Day 18
Have A No News Day

"The man who reads nothing at all is better educated than the man who reads nothing but newspapers."

– Thomas Jefferson, Third President of The United States

Watching or reading the news does more than inform, it can negatively impact you. The news focuses on all the bad and leaves us with the impression that there is more bad than good in the world. That is not true. Millions and millions of good things are happening every moment of every day. It's just that no one is reporting on them.

Take a break from all the negativity and chaos. Allow yourself to dwell on the possibility of goodness in the world. Focusing on positive events and incidents will have a powerful impact on you.

Transformational Actions:

1. Just for today, no news of any kind. Don't read the newspaper, watch the news, listen to the news on the radio, read it on the Internet or have conversations with anyone about the news. Have A No News Day!

2. Write a "good news" article about something that happened to you today.

3. At the end of the day, reflect on your no news day. How was it to have a day off from the news? Did you feel different? How?

Notes:

Day 19
Who Says You Should?

"To be nobody but yourself – in a world which is doing its best, night and day, to make you like everybody else – means to fight the hardest battle which any human being can fight - and never stop fighting."

– e.e. cummings, Poet

The word "should" has judgment and burden in it. I should exercise more, I should eat better, I should read more, I should get a Web site, I should spend more time with the kids; the list goes on and on. We add should after should to our list of "to do's" until we are buried underneath a world of shoulds. Let go of the shoulds by asking, "Who says I should?"

Transformational Actions:

1. Just for today, do things because you *want* to, because the thought of it makes you happy.

2. Let go of the shoulds. When you hear one, either from yourself or someone else, nod, smile and ignore it.

Notes:

Day 20
Share High Points

"Each new day is a blank page in the diary of your life. The secret of success is in turning that diary into the best story you possibly can."

– Douglas Pagels, Author

Let's face it; each of us has had both high point and low point experiences throughout the course of our lives. In fact, in any given week, or day for that matter, we have things that we label "good" or "bad," depending on our own criteria.

Most people tend to focus on the low point experiences and tell those stories over and over again. "Misery loves company," as the saying goes. When you tell a story, you relive it. You feel the experiences all over again, as if it is happening now. Focusing on low point stories drains you of energy and power. Conversely, focusing on high point experiences energizes and empowers you, allowing you to elevate your mood and your performance.

Transformational Actions:

1. Pick a high point experience from your life (see list from Day 2), a time when you felt alive, engaged, and proud of yourself or your accomplishment and share the story with someone. Share the details of the experience, such as when it was, who else was involved and why it was such a high point for you.

2. Ask someone to share a high point experience with you. See Appendix C for sample questions.

3. After telling and listening to the stories, reflect on the experience. What was it like for you to engage in this type of conversation? What did you learn?

Notes:

Day 21
What Do You Really Want?

"There are some people who live in a dream world, and there are some who face reality; and then there are those who turn one into the other."

– Douglas Everett, Canadian Senator

If you could have anything you want, what would it be? If you did not have to figure out how to get it, what would you ask for?

Most people are keenly aware of what they do not want but spend little to no time dwelling on what they *really* want. This creates a world where the best you can hope for is avoiding what you don't want. That is not the same as getting what you *really* want. Begin today to get clear about what you really want.

Transformational Actions:

1. Make a list of what you want. State each item in the affirmative, e.g., if you want to stop arguing with your teenager, write it this way: I want a loving, respectful relationship with my teenager, with open communication.

2. For each item on the list, imagine having it. Do not focus on how. Just imagine if your wish was granted: What would life be like? Who would you have to be?"

Notes:

Day 22
Picture It

"The picture you have in your mind of what you're about will come true."

– Bob Dylan, Singer and Songwriter

"A picture is worth a thousand words." Images are extremely powerful. Pictures have the power to change your experience of life in any given moment. Why do you think so many people put pictures of their loved ones on their desks? It is not to remember what they look like. It is for the experience it brings.

Having pictures or images of what you want is another avenue to getting it. The pictures transport you from the experience you are currently having to the one you want. It helps you to begin to think with the "mind" of having what you want.

Transformational Actions:

1. Review your list from the previous day (Day 21).

2. Go through magazines, online images, etc., and search for images that represent what you want.

3. Make a collage on a poster board of the images you collected.

4. Reflect on the experience: What was it like for you? What did you learn?

Notes:

45

Day 23
Just Play!

"You can discover more about a person in an hour of play than in a year of conversation."

– Plato, Greek Author and Philosopher

We have all gotten too serious. Life has become a series of things to do or accomplish. Playing or having fun has been diminished in value by our "get ahead" culture. In reality, including play in your life is extremely beneficial. Playing for the sake of playing causes a feeling of freedom and joy that is unparalleled.

There is a host of reasons to play more – stress reduction, improved performance, team building – to name a few. Doesn't it strike you as odd that we need good reasons to play?

Just go play!

Transformational Actions:

1.   Play! Pick something, anything, just for fun, not to win. Some examples are hopscotch, tag, dancing to music, going to a video arcade, etc.

2.   Reflect back over the experience. What was it like? What did you learn?

Notes:

Day 24
Discover Your Roots

"Children begin by loving their parents; as they grow older they judge them; sometimes they forgive them."

– Oscar Wilde, Irish Dramatist, Novelist and Poet

One of the biggest transformations of my life was when I realized my mom was a woman first and my mom second. I know this may sound crazy but recognizing my mom as a whole person distinct from our relationship as mother and daughter allowed me to connect with her on an entirely different level.

I got very interested in who she was and in finding out the details of her life. I realized I only knew a small part of her story. Challenging one of your deepest-held "truths," such as who you think your parents are, takes courage but it's worth it.

Transformational Actions:

1. Interview one or both of your parents. If your parents are not alive or well enough to be interviewed, interview someone in their age range or their social circle or, perhaps, someone from their family of origin. See Appendix D for sample interview questions.

2. Listen to learn. Let go of whatever preconceived notions you had about your parents and see what there is to learn.

3. Reflect back on the experience. What was it like to learn about your parent(s)? What did you learn about yourself in the process?

Notes:

Day 25
Forgiveness Part One

"Love yourself — accept yourself — forgive yourself — and be good to yourself, because without you the rest of us are without a source of many wonderful things."

– Dr. Leonardo Buscaglia, Professor and Author

Forgive yourself. It is a simple enough concept but one that is difficult for most people to do. We make it so complicated. Whatever you did or failed to do is likely not as bad as you think. And, by the way, not forgiving yourself doesn't change anything. Whatever happened, happened. It's time to let it go.

What if you did the best you could under the circumstances? What if that "terrible thing" was necessary for your development? What if forgiving yourself is the key to your life moving forward?

This is not about giving yourself carte blanche to go and do whatever you want to others. This is about learning from whatever happened and having compassion for yourself.

Transformational Actions:

1. Forgive yourself. Pick one thing you feel bad about or have not forgiven yourself for and write the story of it. Include what happened, why you did or didn't do whatever, what was the result. Write it all out.

2. Write yourself a letter forgiving yourself.

3. Say out loud, three times, "I forgive myself."

4. If, after completing Step 3, you still have not forgiven yourself, repeat Steps 2 and 3 (i.e., write a new letter) until you have forgiven yourself.

***Bonus: Repeat this exercise for each thing you have not forgiven yourself for.

Notes:

Day 26
Forgiveness Part Two

"Never does the human soul appear so strong and noble as when it foregoes revenge and dares to forgive an injury."

– Reverend E.H. Chapin, Orator and Minister

Forgive someone. Forgiving someone for what they did or did not do does not excuse or condone their behavior. It allows you to move on, to be free.

Holding a grudge is like having one foot stuck in the past, holding you back from living your life. You are allowing the other person to define you. Ask yourself, do you want someone else defining who you are? What if they did the best they could, under the circumstances? What if you do not have all the information about the situation? What if the learning you got out of the situation was necessary for your development? What if forgiving them was the key to your life moving forward?

Or, what if it is none of these things but it's simply time to move on with your life?

Transformational Actions:

1. Pick one person you haven't forgiven. Write the story of what happened from *their* perspective.
2. Write a letter to the person forgiving them. You do NOT have to mail or send this letter to them. This exercise is for you, not for them.
3. Say out loud three times, "(name of person), I forgive you." **Note**: It is NOT necessary to say this to the person, only to yourself.
4. If after completing Step 3 you still feel upset or like you haven't forgiven the person, wait 24 hours and repeat Steps 2 and 3 until you feel free.
   Note: Even attempting to forgive someone is a very generous act. Be gentle with yourself; you are moving in the right direction. Give yourself credit for trying.

***Bonus: Complete this exercise for everyone you have not forgiven.

Notes:

Day 27
Get Physical

"A bear, however hard he tries, grows tubby without exercise."

– "Pooh's Little Instruction Book,"
Inspired by A. A. Milne

Human beings were meant to move around. Think about our ancestors. Hunter-gatherers were constantly moving, looking for food and shelter. Although we have come a long way since then, the fact remains; physical activity is crucial to our well-being.

The benefits of physical activity have been shown in study after study, everything from relieving stress to lowering risks of life-threatening illnesses. In fact, studies have even shown that physical activity works just as well as antidepressants for many individuals suffering from depression. So, today, get your body moving and enhance your physical **and** mental well-being!

Transformational Actions:

1. Your goal today is to do as much physical activity as possible, given your fitness ability. Even if you have a job where you are physically active, your body may have gotten used to that level of activity. Consider adding more or trying a different type of activity.
   Note: If you are **not** in good health or are under a doctor's care, please seek your doctor's approval prior to engaging in any new physical activity.

2. Reflect on how it felt to move your body? What did you learn?

Notes:

Day 28
Be Still

"Your innermost sense of self, of who you are, is inseparable from stillness. This is the I Am that is deeper than name and form."

– Eckhart Tolle, Author and Spiritualist

Life has become so hectic and action-driven we rarely, if ever, find time to be still. We are so busy going from one thing to the next; we have forgotten how important it is to just "be." Stillness has magic and beauty in it. Moments of stillness enliven and engage the deepest parts of us, unleashing our spirit and igniting our imagination. When we quiet our mind and allow ourselves to just be, we have access to true power, the kind that can't be taken away.

Transformational Actions:

1. Reserve 15 minutes in your schedule today for stillness. Find a quiet, secluded place and get comfortable.

2. Let your mind quiet, relax and allow yourself to just be. Each time your mind wanders, focus on your breathing. This will gently pull you back to the present moment.

3. Reflect back over the experience. What did you learn? How were you impacted? What new insights emerged?

Notes:

Day 29
Ask

"You've got to ask. Asking is, in my opinion, the world's most powerful and neglected secret to success and happiness."

– Percy Ross, Philanthropist and Entrepreneur

Somewhere along the way, being a "lone ranger" became revered. Going solo became the ideal. The irony is, it is virtually impossible to accomplish anything alone. There is always someone who contributed to the accomplishment.

Additionally, truly successful people ask for help. Ever watch an awards show? The winners stand at the microphone and thank everyone who helped them achieve their successes. You never hear anyone stand up there and say, "I did it all by myself."

Being free to ask for what you need or want is powerful. Most people love having the opportunity to say yes to helping or contributing to someone's success. Don't you love it when you can help someone? When you know you made a difference in someone's life? Doesn't it feel awesome? Why would you want to rob someone of that feeling? Let people contribute to you and everyone wins.

Transformational Actions:

1. Ask five people for help with something today.

2. Reflect back over the experience. What was it like for you to ask for help? What did you learn about yourself?

Notes:

Day 30
Live It Up!

"Life is not a journey to the grave with the intention of arriving safely in a pretty and well-preserved body, but rather to skid in sideways, thoroughly used up, totally worn out, and loudly proclaiming, 'Wow – what a Ride!' "

– Peter Sage, Entrepreneur and Speaker

Even though we *know* that we have a finite time on this earth and that it could all end tomorrow, we live life as though we have all the time in the world. We put things off, make excuses, and wait for the illusory "someday" that never comes.

The point to life is to LIVE, to do the things that make us happy and fulfilled and to spend as little time as possible on those things that don't.

So, what are you waiting for?

Transformational Actions:

1. Make a list of at least 100 things you want to do in your life. Put a date next to each estimating when you hope to accomplish it.

2. Ask yourself, "Who would I have to be to accomplish those things?" Start being that way NOW!

Notes:

Day 31
Woo Hoo!!

"Life may not be the party we'd hope for but while we are here, we should dance."

– Anonymous

Why are celebrations limited to the big milestones? Why not allow your whole life to be a celebration? Imagine the person you would be if you lived to celebrate. What's the impact you would have on others? What would a life given by celebration look like?

Find reasons to celebrate as often as possible. Celebrate successes large and small. Celebrate failures large and small; after all, you learned something. Celebrate the people who love you and whom you love. Celebrate the people who make your life easier and the ones who challenge you to grow.

Celebrate the wonder of you!

Transformational Actions:

1.   Throw an impromptu party today and celebrate.

2.   Randomly give people standing ovations, just because.

3.   Reflect back on the experience. What was it like to celebrate, just for the sake of celebrating? What did you learn? How can you use this learning in the future?

Notes:

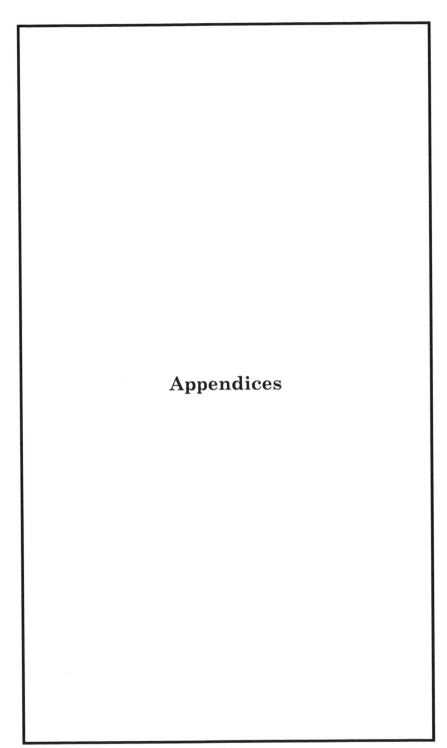

Appendices

Appendix A
Sample Interview Questions

Day 7
Interview Someone You Admire

Sample request:
Hi, my name is _____. I am calling because I am working on a project and I would love to ask you a few questions to learn more about you and how you developed into the person you are. This should take about 15 to 20 minutes. Are you available now or should we schedule a time to talk?

Questions:

1. I admire how you _____, (i.e., communicate directly, empower people, achieved success, etc.) and I wondered how you learned that (or achieved that)?

2. What do you feel is the source of your success?

3. Who have been the key influences on your life?

4. I am sure you, like most people, have had both high points and low points in your life (or career). Would you share a story of an experience that stands out for you as a high point, a time when you felt happy, satisfied, energized, engaged, or proud of yourself and/or your accomplishment?

5. What was it about **you** that made the high point possible?

6. What was it about the **situation** that allowed you to operate at your best?

7. What advice or coaching do you have for someone who wants to accomplish what you have?

Appendix B
Sample Interview Questions

Day 8
Interview Someone Who Admires You

Sample Request:

Hi, I am doing some self-development work to help me discover my strengths and abilities and I wondered if I could ask you a few questions to get your perspective? This should take about 15 to 20 minutes. Are you available now or should we schedule a time to talk?

Questions:

1. What do you think are my top three to five strengths or positive qualities?

2. Can you give me an example of a time when you felt that I was operating at my best?

3. Is there any way that I have contributed to you or your development? If so, would you mind sharing when and how?

4. (Ask this only if this is true for you) I am committed to focusing on and developing my strengths more. Do you have any suggestions or thoughts about how I could do that?

Appendix C
High Point Question Examples

Day 20
High Points

General:
Instead of asking, "How was your _____ (day, weekend, vacation, etc.)?" ask:

"What was the high point of your day/week?" or

"What was the best thing (or your favorite thing) that happened this weekend?" or

"Can you share with me a high point experience from your last vacation?"

For co-worker or colleague:
"_____(Name of person), you have worked at this company for _____. Would you share a story of an experience that stands out for you as a high point, a time when you felt happy, satisfied, energized, engaged or proud of yourself and/or your accomplishment?

For significant other:
We've been together for _____, and we've had our ups and downs. I am curious, what stands out for you as a peak experience, a time when you felt we were really connected and happy? Why was it such a peak experience for you?

For child:
I am committed to being the best _____ (parent, mentor, aunt, uncle, teacher, etc.) I can be. I'd really like for you to share a time when you think I deserved an "A" as a _____ (parent, mentor, aunt, uncle, teacher, etc.) and why?

Appendix D
Sample Interview Questions

Day 24
Discover Your Roots

For parent(s):

1. Before you met and married mom (or dad), what was your life like? What did you do for fun? Where did you work?

2. Did you have a best friend? What was it about them that you liked?

3. What attracted you to mom (or dad)? What do/did you like best about being married to him (or her)?

4. Can you tell me about a time you two shared as a couple before being parents that stands out for you as a high point?

5. What was it like for you to become a parent? What did you like best? What was the biggest challenge?

6. What do you like best about your life now? Do you have a best friend now? What is it about them that you like so much?

7. If you could change one thing about your life, what would it be?

8. If you could live one moment over again, what would it be?

For a relative or friend of your parent(s):

I am interested in discovering more about my parents and I was wondering if you would mind if I asked you some questions to get your perspective?

1. Did you know my mom or dad before they were married? What did they do for fun? For work? (con't next page)

2. Did they have a best friend? What were they like?

3. Do you know what attracted my parents to each other?

4. What did you think about their relationship/marriage?

5. Can you tell me a story about them as a couple before they were parents, when they were particularly happy?

6. Did they like being parents? How do you know? Can you tell me a story that stands out for you as a time they were particularly happy as parents?

7. What do you think mom and dad would most want me to know about them or their lives?

For a non-relative/friend, elderly person who is a parent:

1. Before you met and married your spouse, what was your life like? What did you do for fun? Where did you work?

2. Did you have a best friend? What was that person like?

3. What attracted you to your spouse? What do/did you like best about being married to him or her?

4. Can you share with me a high point experience that you two shared before becoming parents?

5. What was it like for you to become a parent? What did you like best? What was the biggest challenge?

6. What do you like best about your life now? Do you have a best friend now? What is it about them that you like so much?

7. If you could change one thing about your life, what would it be?

8. If you could live one moment over again, what would it be?

About the Author

Lisa Giruzzi

Speaker ♦ Author ♦ Entrepreneur ♦ Consultant

Lisa has always had a strong desire to make a difference in the world. She is fulfilling that desire every day as the owner of her company, Transformational Conversations. Lisa has more than 20 years of experience in coaching and consulting. She has helped thousands to transform their lives, realize their goals, and achieve more satisfaction and fulfillment. Lisa is committed to causing a positive revolution in change.

Lisa is an accomplished speaker; conducting workshops, keynotes and seminars nationwide on topics such as leadership, motivation, effectiveness, communication, team building, networking and customer service. Lisa's programs consistently receive the highest ratings from participants.

Lisa is a founding member of The Creating WE Institute, an international group of critical thinkers who are developing new forms of engagement and innovation in the workplace. Lisa is a co-owner of Appreciative Inquiry Consulting, a global consultancy entirely dedicated to using appreciative, strength-based approaches to organizational change.

Lisa co-hosts "Real Conversations", a topic-driven television talk show dedicated to enhancing the quality of people's lives. The show airs on WNYA, MY4 Albany.

Lisa lives in Albany, New York with her amazing husband, Bill, and Toby, their adorable 9-pound Maltese.

For more resources to transform your life or to sign up for Lisa's newsletter, visit www.TransformationalConversations.com.

31 Days to Transform Your Life
A Daily Action Guide for Increasing Joy
Satisfaction & Fulfillment

Albert Einstein said, "No problem can be solved from the same level of consciousness that created it. We must learn to see the world anew."

Are **YOU** ready to see the world anew?

Do you know others who are ready to see the world anew?

Special Quantity Discounts*

5 - 20	Books	$10.00	each
21 - 50	Books	$8.00	each
51 - 99	Books	$7.00	each
100 - 499	Books	$6.00	each
500 - 999	Books	$5.00	each
1000+	Books	$4.00	each

* Prices do not include shipping and handling

To place an order
visit www.TransformationalConversations.com
or email,
info@TransformationalConversations.com
or call
888-330-8288.

Want more *Transformation?*

Transformational Conversations Presents:

A Transformational Conversation with Lisa Giruzzi, DVD and Action Guide

What great things would **you** achieve if you were unstoppable?

What would be possible if **you** knew the exact formula for achieving greater success?

This provocative and life-altering program will change the way you think about change. The DVD and Action Guide take you on a transformational journey where you will discover new ways of thinking and new openings for action. Your natural creativity, innovation and enthusiasm will be unleashed leading to whole new possibilities.

Examples of what you will learn in A Transformational Conversation with Lisa Giruzzi:

- The ways of thinking that stop you from achieving what you want
- Why focusing on "fixing" yourself actually keeps you stuck
- Ways to leverage what works about you to stay in action
- How to achieve extraordinary results with joy and ease
- The conditions under which **YOU** work best
- How to attain and sustain the positive change you desire
- What's necessary to design the future you *really* want and how to create a personal plan of action to get there

To place an order or for more information on group packages and special quantity discounts, visit www.TransformationalConversations.com or email, info@TransformationalConversations.com or call 888-330-8288.

Speaking Engagements

Lisa provides lively, engaging, life-altering presentations that **wow** audiences by stretching the limits of their thinking. Challenging the status quo and offering a new perspective causes the participants to have insights and "aha's" that create new openings for action leading to immediate results. Delivering dynamic, captivating and transformational presentations is Lisa's specialty.

You'll laugh, you'll think, you'll change!

"Lisa is one of the most innovative and provocative speakers I've ever met. I've never met anyone who can take a subject, and bring it to life the way Lisa does. Just when you think you get the message, she helps you open another door to your mind and get another aha! Refreshing and breathtaking!"

> —Judith E. Glaser; Author of two best selling books: Creating WE and The DNA of Leadership. CEO of Benchmark Communications, Inc. and Founding Member of The Creating WE Institute

If you want your audiences to have breakthroughs in:

- Performance
- Effectiveness
- Productivity
- Motivation
- Satisfaction
- Communication
- Collaboration

Then Lisa Giruzzi is the ideal speaker for your next event!!

To check availability email, info@TransformationalConversations.com or call 888-330-8288. For more information visit, www.TransformationalConversations.com